Stop Renting, Start Buying

8 Steps to Buying A Home After the Housing Crisis

Tonya Brown

www.blisssliferealty.com

Table of Contents

❖

Introduction

❖

What does home ownership mean to you? Perhaps it evokes a sense of security, or is a symbol of success. It may be a haven where you and your family can freely express yourselves. Maybe it's a rung on your ladder in the pursuit of happiness or a cornerstone to building financial wealth. Whatever it means to you the process of getting there may involve excitement, fear, frustration, and uncertainty.

Becoming a homeowner is a journey. Without proper guidance, it can be a nerve-wracking journey. This book will serve as your tour guide. It will provide you with the knowledge to get you to your destination. Whether you're searching for your first home, move up home, or a dream home, this book will provide you with the knowledge needed to achieve your goal. After reading you will know how to choose the proper mortgage program, form a partnership with your ideal real estate agent, and what to expect during the home buying process.

Step 1

❖

Develop a Homeowner Mindset

The recession and housing crisis left many of us believing that we would never be able to afford to purchase a home or that we would never own a home again. We believe that that if we don't have at least 20% for the down payment, we can not purchase a home, that information is incorrect.

While it is true that most of your financial gurus suggest that you save 20% down payment before buying a home. That advice is not always feasible, for today's consumer. The truth in today's terms is you can use a smaller down payment to buy a home and be building equity during the time it would have taken you to save the 20% down payment. According to a 2015 survey by Trulia, it can take from 5.1 years in some southern states to 29.2 years in coastal states such as California to save the 20% down payment. The average mortgage is 30 years, so you could buy with a smaller down payment and have your home paid off in the same amount of time it would take you to save the 20%.

Why rent when you can own? The real cost of renting at $800 per month with a 6% rental increase per year means you pay $126,552, over a ten year period. You could almost afford to payoff a home for that amount!

The reality of today's market is with moderate home prices, low-interest rates, and the many down payment assistance programs now is an optimal time to buy.

Before starting the process it's important to determine what your goals are, and how owning a home will fit into those goals. This decision requires you to evaluate the long-term and pros and cons of homeownership.

The Pros, Cons, and Benefits of Homeownership- There are both some emotional and personal aspects of your home buying decision.

- Homeownership becomes the opportunity to establish some roots and become part of a community.

- It can make you feel stable and secure, which in turn can make you feel more grounded as you build your career.

- It allows you the freedom to do as you please without asking a landlord's permission.

- Most important it is a foundation for enhancing your personal wealth. You will build equity by (1) making your mortgage payments and (2) as your home grows in value.

Don't spend time worrying about your home losing value. Real estate runs in a cycle, it may go down but always rises again. The best thing you can do is make good financial decisions during an upturn and not use your home equity as an ATM machine.

Your biggest con is most likely your ability to save a down payment of 3.5% to 20% and pay closing cost of an additional 3.5% to 4%. Many times these cost exceed the cash outlay needed to rent. However, this is not the case in all locales. The many down payment assistance programs currently available helps turn this con into a pro.

Homeownership involves other financial gains, your mortgage interest is tax deductible, as well as some of the closing cost. Any points paid to lower your mortgage interest rate are also deductible for the year they incurred. Talk to your tax advisor for in-depth tax advice.

So let's recap your advantages to homeownership:

Equity- A portion of your monthly mortgage payment goes toward building equity (value) in your home. This equity can serve as collateral for a loan that allows you to convert equity to cash.

Tax Breaks- Property taxes and mortgage payments are tax deductible on your federal income tax return. This often is a life saver to singles and older people without children at home, as it is often the lifeline that prevents them from owing Uncle Sam.

Investment- Your new home is usually the single greatest asset in your portfolio. Its value appreciates over the long term. Many retirees sell their home and downsize to a less expensive home and use their profits to supplement retirement income. Even if you're not ready to retire consider that if you live in your home 5 years or less when you move you have a chance of making a profit (I've made a profit on homes I lived in less than 2 years).However when you rent for 5 years at say $1,000, you've paid $60,000 towards your landlords mortgage and all he's going to give you is a sorry to see you go and maybe part of your deposit.

Now that we know the advantages of homeownership let's jump into the additional steps you will need to take to buy that home.

Step 2

❖

Get Pre-Approved

Home buying does not begin with house hunting unless you have all cash and do not need a mortgage loan. The first thing you need to do is get your financing in place. I can't begin to tell you the number of people who try to avoid this step. You simply can not, it is the only way to actually know whether you are financially capable of making a home purchase. If you are not ready at this time, at least you now know what you need to do to structure a game plan to position yourself for homeownership in the future.

Realtors can not even begin to choose homes to show you without knowing your home buying power.

Pre-approval vs. Prequalified- A prequalification is simply the lender certifying that you prequalify for a loan based on a credit report and very little documentation. In today's market, most sellers will not accept a prequalification letter.

With a pre-approved loan, the lender has agreed to grant you a loan without you yet committing to buy a specific property.

To get pre-approved you will fill out a full mortgage application, you may be required to pay a small application fee or credit report fee. The lender will need:

General

- Non-expired Government ID and Social Security Number.
- Name and complete address for past 2 years of residence.

Income

- Employment history, including names, addresses, phone numbers for the past 2 years.

- Copies of your most recent pay stubs and W-2 forms (past 2 years).

- Verification of other income (social security, child support, retirement).

- Copies of signed tax returns including all schedules (past 2 years).

- Social Security & Pension Award letters.

- If you have rental property income: Copies of all signed lease agreements.

Assets

- Copies of all bank statements from checking/savings accounts (past 2 months).

- CD certificates and statements for retirement accounts (most recent 2 months or quarterly statement).

- Gift funds will need gift letter of proof of gift.

Creditors

- Credit cards (current balances and monthly payments).

- Installment loans (car, student, etc.).

- Mortgage loans (property address, lender information, account numbers, monthly payment and balance owed on all properties presently owned or sold within the last 2 years). Bring proof of sale for properties sold.

- Childcare expense/support (name, address, phone number). [VA loans only]

Other

- Bankruptcy – bring discharge and schedule of creditors.

- Adverse credit – bring letters of explanation.

- Divorce – bring your Divorce Decrees, property settlements, quitclaim deeds, modifications, etc.

- VA only – bring Form DD214 and Certificate of Eligibility.

- Retires – bring retirement and/or Social Security Award Letter.

The lender may require additional information based on your individual circumstances.

The upside to this is unless you want to you don't need to see your lender in person. This process can now be handled via online and email, and lenders can usually have your pre-approved within 24-48 hours.

Some other pre-approval facts:

- Getting pre-approved for a certain amount does not mean you have to borrow that amount (you can buy a lower house). However, the pre-approved amount is your maximum so you can not go over that amount unless you plan to pay the difference in cash.

- Pre-approval letters have an expiration date. If your letter expires before you, find a home your lender will need to recertify you. The lender will require recent paystubs and bank statements for recertification.

- Home sellers see you as a serious buyer.

Down Payment: How much do I need?-The mortgage lender will give you a mortgage, but a down payment will be required. We always talk about down payment, but the reality is you will need both down payment and closing cost to purchase your home.

There is a wide variety of loan programs with minimum down payment requirements ranging from 3% to 20%, and closing cost can run an average of another 3.5% to 4%. There is also a wide variety of options available to assist first-time homebuyers and those who have not owned a home in the last 3 years with the funds for down payment and closing cost.

Most home buyers neglect the state and local down payment assistance programs because they believe these programs are for low-income home buyers, when, in fact, most programs benefit middle-income consumers.

Today's down payment assistance programs are relatively easy to obtain, there are not many hoops to jump through. Most down payment assistance programs will require you to attend a home buyer education class. The class is usually one-day and some programs accept the online course. Many of the programs assist with a percentage of the down payment and closing cost, and others provide flat amounts. In some instances, programs can be combined. Buyers who utilize these programs can often get into a home for as little as $1500-2000 out of pocket, which in some states can be less than the cost to rent an apartment.

Get a Home Within Your Means- The excitement of buying a new home can cause you to lose your head. Sometimes when you fall in love with a house, common sense jumps right out the window.

Although you will get yourself pre-approved early in the process, you must also consider what fits comfortably in your personal budget. This is necessary because pre-approval is based on gross income, but mortgages and bills are actually paid with your net pay(take home dollars). For example based on your pre-approval you may be able to obtain a mortgage with a monthly payment of $1300 which results in you being able to purchase a home with a $200,000 price tag, however $1300 may not be a comfortable fit for your personal budget. Suppose you feel more comfortable with $1000 monthly payment, which

– 10

results in a home with a $150,000 price tag. A $50,000 higher price tag can make a difference to the home you buy, but you must keep your head and make the best financial decision for yourself and your family. Remember your buying a home as a long-term investment, but do not want to go broke in the near future.

Your Credit and Credit Scores- First and foremost, credit scores are not all there is. Lenders review your overall credit history, not the scores only. Here is the skinny on the basics mortgage lenders look for when approving a home loan.

- Mortgage lenders require a minimum credit score. The average required is 620.

- Higher scores typically result in better rates, thus lower payments. Credit scores of 720 and higher generally qualify for the best rates.

- Minimum of 3 trade lines active for at least 6 months, preferably at least 1 credit line will be an installment loan. (You do not need a lot of credit lines, as more credit lines equal more debt, and the more debt you have decreases your buying power.)

- If your credit lines are less than 6 months old, you may not have a score yet.

- Preferably no collections, judgments, bankruptcy, foreclosure, short sale, or tax liens, but if so there are special circumstances to deal with these issues.

Collections/Judgments- Mortgage lenders may require you to payoff your collection and/or judgment accounts prior to final loan approval or at closing. There are few exceptions to this rule, however, small collections of less than $1,000 and more than 2 years old may sometimes be waived at the lenders discretion.

Tax Liens- Will be required to be paid off and released or you will need to have a payment plan in place for at least 6 months with on time payments with the tax authority agreeing to subordinate to the lender's mortgage. This is because tax authorities are the only entities that have the power to overstep your mortgage company and foreclose on your home.

Buying after Bankruptcy- All is not lost after bankruptcy here are the facts for buying after a bankruptcy:

For FHA Loan Programs-

Chapter 7

- 2 years with re-established credit paid as agreed and no derogatory credit after the bankruptcy.

- Less than 2 years but not less than 12 months if bankruptcy was caused by acceptable extenuating circumstances and buyer has since exhibited a documented ability to manage finances (talk to your lender for information regarding extenuating circumstances)

Chapter 13

- 1-year payout under the bankruptcy has elapsed and your payment performances have been satisfactory and all required payments are made one time. You will need to obtain approval from the bankruptcy trustee.

- If the Chapter 13 has been dismissed, then the waiting period is the same as the Chapter 7 waiting period.

For Conventional Loan Programs-

Chapter 7

- 4 years from discharge date

Chapter 13

- 2 years from discharge date

- 4 years from dismissal date

Re-entry Buyers (Short Sales and Foreclosures)- There is so much misinformation surrounding these subjects, but the fact of the matter is there is life after short sale and foreclosure. You can once again be a homeowner. Below you will find the waiting times for short sale and foreclosure. Both short sale and foreclosure will have a devasting effect on your credit. You will need to reestablish your credit prior to your home purchase.

Short Sale

For FHA Loan Programs-

- 2 years from the date the sale closed.

- No waiting period if there have been no late payments on any mortgages and consumer debts within the 12 months preceding the short sale AND they are not taking advantage of a declining market.

- A minimum of 12 months if the short sale was a result of an Economic Event (talk to your lender to see what qualifies as an economic event)

For Conventional Loan Programs-

- *Applications received after August 16, 2014- 4 years from the date of the sale

Foreclosures/Deed instead of Foreclosure

- 3 years from date foreclosure were completed

- Less than 2 years, but not less than 12 months with acceptable extenuating circumstances

What is a mortgage loan and How do I qualify?

A mortgage is a debt secured by the collateral of real estate property, that the borrower is obligated to pay back within a set period of time.

Most lenders require that your monthly mortgage payment is in a maximum range between 29-36% of your gross monthly income. Your mortgage will typically include the following:

- Principal on the loan (P)

- Interest on the loan (I)

- Property taxes (T)

- Homeowners Insurance (I)

This is what is called PITI and your total monthly PITI and all debt (from installments to revolving charge accounts) should be no more than a maximum of 36-45% of your gross monthly income. The key factors to determine your ability to secure a mortgage are: Credit, Income, Assets, and Debt Ratios.

Choosing the Right Mortgage For You- Mortgages are not one size fits all. You will not qualify for all mortgage programs. Mortgage programs have guidelines and specifications, so what may seem simple can have one small piece missing and cause you not to qualify. You need to choose the mortgage that is right for you and your finances at the time you purchase your home.

The basic types of mortgage programs are 15,20, and 30-year mortgages. The most common today are 30-year mortgages. These mortgage program types may be FHA, VA, Conventional or Private/ Hard Money.

65Major banks are not the only financial institutions that can grant a mortgage loan. Credit unions and direct mortgage lenders also grant mortgages. Keep in mind banks often have the most stringent set of guidelines. Therefore, you may sometimes not qualify via your local bank but still be able to qualify with another lender, which is why it is best to check more than one resource.

It is common practice for a bank or lender to grant your initial loan then sell your loan to a larger bank or lender. When this happens and it will happen, the terms covering your original loan will remain intact. Your loan is a contract bounded for honoring by whoever buys it. Be familiar with your contract terms.

Fixed Rate Vs Adjustable Rate-Mortgage programs vary on payment plans, distinguished by interest rate and payment duration. The most common are fixed rate mortgages, where the interest rate remains unchanged.

Another common option is the adjustable rate. Whereby the interest rate changes annually or after a specified time.

There are also hybrid mortgages that are a combination of fixed and adjustable rates. These may be fixed for a set period and then become fixed. There are numerous combinations.

In a low-interest rate environment, such as today's market, it is best to obtain a fixed rate mortgage. Interest rates change daily so you actually will not know your rate until it is locked in with your lender.

Adjustable Rate Mortgage-interest rate changes at preset intervals, indicative of current market index movements. Theis type of mortgage is suitable for someone who:

- Does not have intentions to stay in the home for an extended period of time.

- If you plan to renovate and sell the in a short period of time.

- Seeking a lower payment for a brief period of time.

Fixed Rate Mortgage- has a fixed interest rate throughout the duration of the loan term. With a fixed rate:

- You have a predictable, steady payment
- This best if you plan to live in the home for a longer duration of time.

Combined Mortgage- most commonly entails a fixed rate over a specific duration of time then beginning to adjust yearly. This mortgage can suit you if:

- You are planning to live in the home for a set duration and sell before the mortgage becomes adjustable.
- You are planning to refinance or reevaluate your loan and finances before the mortgage becomes adjustable.

Mortgage Program Types- As mentioned earlier there are various mortgage types with the most common being FHA, VA, Conventional, and Private/Hard Money. One type is not necessarily better than another as they each serve different consumer bases. Thay all offer either fixed, adjustable, or combo loan programs.

FHA- is a mortgage loan insured by the US Federal Housing Administration. FHA loans are provided by FHA-approved lenders. They are designed for low to moderate income borrowers who are unable to make large down payments.With FHA loans, you pay for mortgage insurance known aka MIP. This insurance does not benefit you as the consumer, rather it protects the lender from loss should you default on the loan.

FHA loan facts:

- You may obtain an FHA loan with less than perfect credit. Typically FHA will allow you to get a loan with a 3.5% down payment with a credit score of 580 or higher. However, keep in mind that the lenders (banks, credit unions, direct lenders, etc.)

each has their own credit overlays, and there are very few that will approve a loan at less than 620 credit score.

- FHA also allows a loan to those with a credit score between 500-579. However, you will need a 10% down payment. It is difficult to find lenders that actually administer these loans in today's climate.

- Your down payment does not need to come from your personal savings. Other allowed down payment sources are: a gift from a family member and/or a grant from state or local government down payment assistance programs.

- Home sellers, builders, and lenders are allowed to pay your closing cost up to 3%. If the lender pays your closing cost, they will charge you a slightly higher interest rate.

- FHA is not a lender, but rather an insurer. You will need to get your loan through an FHA approved lender. Not all FHA-approved lenders offer the same interest rates and costs. Costs, rates, services and underwriting standards will vary among lenders, so it is important to shop around.

- FHA loans require a 2 part mortgage insurance premium. The first part is the upfront premium, it is paid once at loan inception. The current upfront premium is 1.75% of the loan amount. The upfront premium is typically financed into the loan. The second part is the annual premium and it is paid monthly by being added to your mortgage payment. This premium varies based on the length of the loan, the amount borrowed and the initial loan to value. Below are the current FHA annual premiums (based on the date of this publication)

  - 30-year loan with down payment (or equity) of less than 5%: 0.85%

  - 30-year loan with down payment (or equity) of 10% or

more: 0.80%

- 15-year loan with down payment (or equity) of less than 10%: 0.70%

- 15-year loan with down payment (or equity) of 10% or more: 0.45%

FHA has a special loan product for buyers who need cash to make home repairs. This loan is called the FHA 203K. There are two types of 203K loans; regular and streamlined. The most popular of the two is the 203K streamline which allows you to finance up to $35,000 in nonstructural repairs such as painting, flooring, and replacing cabinets and fixtures.

Conventional- A conforming conventional loan is a mortgage with terms and conditions that meet the funding criteria of Fannie Mae and Freddie Mac.

Conventional Loan facts:

- Conventional loans have more stringent guidelines than FHA loan programs. Conventional loans require a minimum 620. Fico score and many lenders credit overlays require a minimum 640 Fico score.

- Require 5% down payment. However, there are programs that require as little as 3% down payment. The 3% down payment are not always available.

- Fannie Mae and Freddie Mac are not lenders or insurers. Rather they guarantee the purchase of loans that meet conforming guidelines.

- Conventional loans require private mortgage insurance aka PMI. Anytime a buyer makes a down payment of less than 20%. Just as with MIP, PMI does not benefit the consumer but insures the lender of loss in case of default. PMI insurers have their own set of guidelines that must be passed for the loan to be insured, so if a loan cannot be insured the loan will be denied.

- Sellers and Lenders are allowed to pay up to 3% of your closing cost. The lender will charge a slightly higher interest rate when paying your closing cost.

VA- a mortgage loan backed the Department of Veteran Affairs. VA loans are made by banks, savings&loans, or mortgage companies to eligible veterans for the purchase of a home which they must owner-occupy.

VA Loan Facts:

- VA is not a lender, the VA guaranty protects the lender against loss up to the amount guaranteed by the VA.

- There is no maximum VA loan guaranty, but lenders generally limit VA loans to $417,000. Just because there is no maximum guaranty and lenders allow up to 417,000, this does not mean this Is the amount you can borrow. You will still need to get pre-approved to find out your home buying power based on your credit, income, and asset information.

- VA loans do not require a down payment (unless required by the lender or the purchase price is more than the reasonable value of the property)

- A 2.15% funding fee is required for first-time users and can be financed into the loan. The funding fee is 3.3% for second-time users.

- VA loans do not have mortgage insurance premiums (i.e. no MIP or PMI).

- Sellers and Lenders are allowed to pay up to 3% of the buyer's closing cost.

- VA loans can be used by a Veterans widow/widower provided she/he has does not remarry.

Private/Hard Money-These loans are provided by private lenders. They usually require at least 30% down payment and have high-interest rates. These loans are used primarily by investors and are not the best choice for first time home buyers.

Mortgage Brokers, Banks, and Direct Lenders

Mortgage Brokers- The primary function of a mortgage broker is to act as an intermediary between you and your lender. A broker does not originate or service loans like a bank or direct lender. A mortgage brokers principal advantage is having knowledge and relationships with various lenders. Brokers tend to have a wider knowledge base regarding available loan products. Brokers offer a more hands on approach and are usually more easily accessible to answer their clients questions and ease fears.

Brokers not only help you handle your home financing at the present but can also help you achieve long-term financial goals. Just like insurance and other financial vehicles as life changes so do your mortgage needs. A good mortgage broker will keep you updated on industry trends and financing options long after the purchase of your home closes.

Banks- Major banks are the most common place a consumer goes for a loan. Although you may pay a few hundred dollars less initially obtaining a loan through the bank loan officer, however, you may wind up paying more over the life of the loan. Banks only offer their own products it does not necessarily mean that it is the loan product that best fits your financial needs.

Bank officers are not paid to be familiar with the competition's products. Therefore, they can only assist you with their banks offerings. If you are declined by a bank, it does not necessarily mean you can not purchase a home it may be that you do not qualify for their products.

Shop around and keep in mind, banks are usually the most stringent with their underwriting guidelines.

Direct Mortgage Lenders- Direct lenders are retail lenders that issue mortgages directly to individual consumers.

They may originate the loans themselves or via a mortgage broker. Much like banks direct lenders typically offer only their own mortgage products.

Banks, credit unions, and direct lenders may have wholesale divisions where they offer their products via mortgage brokers. The brokers are provided with discount pricing so that they can be competitive. With this being the case, brokers can often provide a better overall deal for home buyers and mortgage borrowers.

Lease Purchase/Rent to Own

Lease purchase, lease with an option to buy, rent to own it's all the same.

In the aftermath of the recession, many have been looking at creative solutions to purchase a home. Well, let's just say creative does not always equal smart.

Here is an overview of how the lease purchase/rent to own process works:

- The leasee/renter pays an upfront option fee, which guarantees the leasee/renter the option to purchase the home for a specified amount of time, usually 1 to 5 years.

- The option fee can be as little as an amount equal to the rent, or as much as 10% of the asking sales price.

- The leasee/renter agrees to a monthly rental rate slightly above fair market value. The amount above fair market value is credited towards your down payment in an eventual sale.

- During the contract period, the homeowner (landlord/seller) cannot sell the home to anyone else.

- You do not own the home until you complete the purchase at the specified time until then you are just renting.

- The purchase price is set within the contract, and the leasee/renter will purchase the home at the preset price whether the home value goes up or down.

- The contract usually contains clauses that are in the homeowner's (sellers) favor such as: disallowing late (even 1 day) payments from counting toward an eventual sale; the renter is almost always responsible for maintenance and repairs.

- At the agreed upon date, the leasee/renter can choose to buy the home at the original listed price minus the equity they have built via the rental credits.

- If you choose to purchase the home, you will still need to obtain standard financing (FHA, Conventional, etc.), which means you need to qualify for a mortgage loan.

- Mortgage lenders require the rent credits to be held in an escrow account to count towards the down payment. If this has not been handled properly, your loan will be declined.

- The mortgage lender has to agree that the base rent was at fair market value, and the amount you were credited monthly was actually extra. This determination is made by an appraiser. If the lender determines you did not pay fair market value, they will not allow you to use the extra credits towards the down payment.

- When it's time to purchase if you have not addressed the issues that prevented you from buying in the first place albeit credit or finances, etc. You will not be in a position to secure a mortgage loan. Thus, you will not be able to purchase the home.

- If you decide not to purchase the home or you are unable to secure financing, the homeowner (landlord) can evict you and **keep all your payments**.

If you are not ready to buy a home right now, instead of lease purchase/ renting to own.Set up a separate savings account and save the money on your own with no risk of losing it.

Bottomline: Lease purchase/ lease with an option to buy/rent to own or whatever name it is called by is not a good idea for you as a consumer. But is a pretty good deal for a homeowner (landlord).

Step 3

--- ❖ ---

The Benefits of A Great Real Estate Agent

Buying a home can be much like taking a flight. You may fly comfortably through the sky, but at some point you may experience some turbulence. You don't feel so afraid when you have a flight crew that is providing excellent service and make you feel you can trust their abilities to get you to your destination safely. Your real estate agent is the captain of your crew and you should feel you can trust him or her to guide you through your home buying experience.

As your captain, the ideal agent will play 3 key roles in your home buying journey. He/she will act as your consultant, negotiator, and transaction manager.

Consultant: As your consultant a professional agent will layout a game plan for helping you to find your home while keeping in mind both your needs and wants. Your agent will consider what will work best for you and your family. Your agent should communicate with you regularly. Keep you focused on homes that satisfy your needs, while at the same time attempting to meet your wants. All while keeping you within your budget. Your agent should proficient in their knowledge of real estate and the home buying process and educate you along the way. Your agent should provide solutions to any obstacles you may encounter.

Negotiator: Once you have located a home and would like to make an offer, your real estate agent then needs to slip into the role o negotiator. As a negotiator, your agent, will research and review recent sell activity in the area, as well as the condition of the home. Your agent will utilize this information to assist you in making an informed decision when deciding how much to offer. As your negotiator, your agent should be willing to treat your money as if it is their own. Your agent should go to bat for you to get you the best price possible. Once you have a binding purchase contract, there are times when your agent will need to negotiate to keep your transaction on track and get you to closing.

Transaction Manager: Buying a home is not as simple as looking for a home and signing a contract. There are several moving parts working simultaneously to make the process happen.A typical real estate transaction will involve 12-15 people (sometimes more) and your real estate agent has to manage them all. Your real estate agent has to coordinate all parties and communications to ensure all disclosures, inspections, repairs, loan approvals, legal documentation, etc., are completed timely so that you meet your contractual obligation to close in a timely manner.

A lot of your real estate agent's work is done behind the scene. Below is a list of some of the task your real estate agent will perform on your behalf when representing you as the buyer:

- Pursue the interests of the Buyer Client

- Enter into Buyer Agency Agreement

- Helps explain the process, sequence, contracts, mortgages, pre-approvals, closings

- Reviews Closing Costs on an HUD-1 Estimated Worksheet

- Explain Earnest Money Deposits, Escrow, and Default

- Listen and answer questions

- Shows client homes that client found on the internet or agent found doing research

- Generates comparable data for Buyer to understand current

pricing

- Reviews and explains the Regional Sales Contract, Addendums, and Contingencies

- Complete offer to purchase with Buyer and presents any offer to Seller or Seller's Agent

- Explains counter-offers, makes sure contract is ratified

- Helps schedule home inspections, radon tests, termite inspections, etc.

- On new homes, schedule option selections

- Gets contract to mortgage lender and settlement company

- Gives buyer insight into homeowners insurance, locking mortgage rate

- Makes sure appraisal has been ordered within time frame

- Reviews Home Owner's Association or Condo Documents and presents them to Buyer for review

- Contacts Title Company for updates, such as title or survey issues

- Contacts mortgage lender to make sure loan is in process and provide any missing information

- Helps resolve Buyer or Seller issues that may delay closing or void the contract

- Schedules contractors to evaluate or any repair issues from inspections

- On new homes, contact builders rep for estimated closing date

- Schedule closing time, walk-through inspections, walk-through issues

- Review "rent-back" agreement if necessary

- Make sure Home Owner's Insurance Policy is in place

- Confirm with Title Company that Buyer's loan documents and Seller documents are ready to be signed

- Ensure Buyer has certified Funds for amount due at closing, get proper wiring instructions

- Provide accurate contacts for utility transfers

- Be available at closing

Full-Time vs. Part-Time Real Estate Agent

Your home is likely the most expensive purchase you will make, yet many home buyers give little thought to choosing an agent.

You want to select an agent who is actively involved in the real estate business on a daily basis. The bulk of an agent's job is performed after a contract has been signed. The agent needs to make sure the sale closes. Real estate transactions are processed during business hours. Therefore, if your part time agent is at their other full-time job during business hours, how can he/she perform the duties required to close your transaction promptly. Your agent performing their duties during the evening after they get home from their day job may cause your transaction to be delayed.

By no means will I state that all agents are the same. In real estate experience doesn't always equate to knowledge. You need to find an agent capable of performing the duties needed. Here is a list of 11 questions you should ask before hiring a real estate agent:

1. ***Can you send me some information about yourself?*** Look for professionalism and consistency. What are their professional accomplishments?

2. ***How do you approach your work?*** Look for a businessperson that has a strategy and a team to work with.

3. ***How many homes have you closed in the past year?*** Look for an agent who is active in your area and at the top of their industry. Part-time agents are simply unable to keep up with the ever-changing demands of the market. A good rule of thumb is a minimum of 10-15 transactions. Why settle for less?

4. ***What is the dollar volume of homes you have sold in the last year?*** Beware of agents who use their company status vs. their own.

5. ***How long have you been in business?*** Longevity in the industry does not always mean success. However, look for an agent that has been in the business for a minimum of three years. The fall-out ratio for agents in the business less than 3 years is over 80%. While experience is important, accomplishments are more significant. How many homes have they sold in the area you are looking?

6. ***Do you have a personal assistant or other support staff working for you?*** Most top agents employ (out of their own pocket) an assistant or staff. It is imperative that the agent has support to take care of the details of the transaction. How can your agent be actively showing homes to clients and working on the details of your closing at the same time? Things will fall through the cracks and that could cause critical problems for you.

7. ***What will you do keep me informed?*** Do you want daily or weekly reports from your agent? Will the agent be able to meet these expectations? Determine how much communication you want, and then find an agent who will give you the attention and time you want and deserve.

8. ***Can you provide me with further resources I may need?*** The best agents have built strong relationships with their "Teams" and can often get expedient service or be able to "cash in a favor" for you should a crunch or problem arise.

9. ***Can you give me some references from other clients you have worked with?*** Don't be afraid to ask for references. An agent who provides raving fan service and is proud of their work will be happy to provide references.

10. ***What is the best way for me to get in touch with you?*** You should know exactly how to get through to your agent or assistant.

11. ***Are you a fiduciary? And how will you represent my best interests?*** Absolutely do not hire someone that you don't believe will represent YOUR best interests at all times. Have your agent give you examples of how they represent their client. Remember that finding the home is the easy part, true representation begins when you sign a contract and continues through negotiation and closing. Ask around for horror stories and you will find that they don't involve the home search BUT after the contract was signed!

Realtor Commissions and What They Mean To You- Real estate agent fees and commissions are surely a topic worthy of discussion. Here is a simple universal explanation of real estate fees. In short, you (the buyer) generally pays 0 to a very small fee.

- Real Estate commissions are paid once the purchase is complete.

- Real Estate commissions are paid by the seller (unless you agree to something different in the contract). The seller is paying for someone to bring a buyer to them.

- Commissions are negotiable and generally works something

like this- the seller agrees to pay his agent (listing agent) a commission usually based on a percentage of the sales price and the listing agent agrees to split the commission fee with the buyer's agent.

- Some buyer's agent charges a small administration fee to cover the cost of administration cost and gas, in case the buyer does not end up purchasing a property.

Step 4

❖

Find Your Home

As a homebuyer armed with a good real estate agent and a pre-approval letter, you are prepared to begin your house hunting journey. Sellers will take you seriously as a buyer and be excited to show their home.

While you can search for homes online, your agent still possesses the most up to date information about what's available. The big online real estate databases are nothing more than advertising vehicles for agents and are not always updated in a timely manner.

Your Future Neighborhood

While you can search for homes online, your agent still possesses the most up to date information about what's currently available. The big online real estate databases are nothing more than advertising vehicles for agents and are not always updated in a timely manner.

Your agent can provide you with information about neighborhoods in which you're interested such as school information, walkability scores, and demographics.

Househunting ultimately begins with the neighborhood and there are several factors to take into account. When considering neighborhoods, the most common considerations are the following:

- Location-Proximity- how far are your from your workplace, schools, grocery, hospitals, churches, airports, parks, gyms, libraries, shopping malls, restaurants, children activity centers, recreational areas, and other landmarks.

- Desirability of the area and depreciation of property value, which implies whether or not the houses in the community are holding their value.

- Lifestyle considerations, such as walkability, nightlife, sports, and fitness centers, club memberships, beauty and barber salons.

- Potential for customization for future expansion/deconstruction thru its design and layout.

HOA-An HOA is a Homeowners Associations. Some neighborhoods are part of an HOA. Consider whether you want to live in a community with an HOA, as HOA's stipulate monthly or yearly dues, which need to be considered in your budget. Depending on who you talk to an HOA can be considered a positive or negative. Here are some things the HOA may stipulate:

- Community Appearance- Generally homes within an HOA must meet certain standards of upkeep set by the association or face a fine. Some HOAs even have a board that needs to approve any changes you make to the exterior, or notes about cars and vehicles parked on the property.

- Recreational Amenities- While not all HOAs offer amenities most provide a range of amenities such as a community clubhouse, swimming pools, tennis courts, walking trails, etc. reserved for use by the community residents only.

- Low Maintenance- Typically common areas are maintained by the association. The association may sometimes handle other services also.

Your Future Home

The number one thing to remember when house hunting is there are no perfect homes. You will need to be open to compromise sometimes on the house itself other times it may be the neighborhood. Whatever it is there will come a point in time when you will need to compromise.

Your real estate can help you identify when and how to compromise, as well as show you alternatives so you can make an informed decision.

Buy What You Need Not What You Want

When you're searching for a home, you should begin by organizing your needs and wants. The home features you want are not always the same ones you need. With all the house hunting television shows it is easy to be awestruck by the razzle dazzle aspect of finding a home. Who doesn't love looking at marble and granite countertops, wood floors, and massive suites? But before you start feeding your indulgences make sure a home meets your practical needs. Needs are what you and your family actually need to live daily in the home, such as square footage. For example, you may need 3 bedrooms and 2 baths in 1500 square feet or would your require a bit more space to accommodate hobbies, kids toys or a business. On the other hand does your family of 4 actually require 3 bedrooms and 2 baths in 4000 square feet, or will you be busting your budget trying to keep up with the heating and cooling cost. Needs are also things for which you are willing to sacrifice and willing to pay more. It is also good to consider that the average American lives in their home for 7-9 years, so you want to make sure to consider any life changes you may soon make such as starting a family.

Wants Are Things You Can Add or Change – Wants are things you'd like to have but don't necessarily need. Wants are also things that you can easily add or change on your own such as paint colors, carpet, countertops, or the current owner décor.

A good real estate agent may have you complete a house hunting checklist and assist with a reality check in determining the difference between needs and wants.

New Home vs. Existing Home- A new home is exactly that: a brand new home that has never been lived in before. An existing home is an existing home that has been previously owned and lived in.

According to a 2014 Trulia survey almost twice as many people (41%) prefer new homes to those who prefer existing homes (21%).

New homes typically cost about 20% more than similar existing homes (e.g. square footage, beds, baths, etc.) in the same neighborhood. Once you move in there can also be some additional cost, in some states new homes are not completely landscaped and this is an expense for the owner. You need to consider your budget in these instances as landscaping can be expensive in some regions.

The top reasons some people prefer new homes are:

- They have modern features, such as bigger closets, open floor plans, newer style kitchens, or prewired for modern technology.

- Spend less on maintenance and repairs.

- Homes can be customized prior to construction.

The top reasons for those who prefer existing homes are:

- They prefer a home with characters such as original hardwood floors, molding, and ornate details.

- They prefer living in an established neighborhood.

Bottom line, you may choose to look at both new and existing homes. However, never purchase a new home directly from the builder without your own real estate agent to represent you in the transaction as builder's contracts lean heavily in the builder's favor. You need your own representation.

Another option to consider is an existing home in need of repairs or rehab. You can almost always snag a better deal with a house requiring repairs and will have the ability to actually customize the home to your specification. If you choose this option, locate a realtor who specializes in working with these types of properties, as they require specialized knowledge.

House Hunting How To's- Here are some tips to assist you in your house hunting:

- Narrow Down your listings- choose your top 3-5 to view during a showing appointment. Viewing to many homes on one day will serve to do nothing more than cause confusion. If you do not find a house after viewing3-5, then schedule another showing appointment.

- Always utilize your needs vs. wants checklist so that you can break down the home to basics.

- Take pictures to assist you in remembering what you liked about the home.

- If you have viewed 15 or more homes and have not found one to make an offer. You and your agent need to reevaluate your needs and wants. You and your agent should be on the same page.

- **Stick to your budget**- You and your real estate agent can start searching for homes within your budget. You do not have to spend up to your pre-approval maximum. If you can find a lower home that meets your needs, it is ok to do so. A good agent will not pressure you to spend over your budget. Alternatively, if you want to consider a home outside your pre-approved amount keep in mind you will more than likely need to make up the difference with cash out of pocket. Remember, your budget is not just your pre-approved loan amount you need to consider not only mortgage payments but all housing expenses as well as your other debts.

- Sometimes you may not gel well with your real estate agents and may need to find another agent. That's ok if you are in a state that utilizes a buyer agency contract ask nicely to cancel. Most agents will not want to work with you if you don't wish to work with them. If you find that you go through 2-3 agents, it's not the agents it's you and you will need to reevaluate your needs.

Step 5

❖

Making An Offer

Prior to going into the specifics of this step, below you will find a few key definitions that will give you understanding in this part of the process:

Purchase Agreement (Contract)/Offer to Purchase

The purchase agreement (contract) is a legally binding document indicating the amount of your offer. It also spells out the terms of the agreement such as what fixtures and/or appliances remain, when inspections should be completed, when disclosures are to be exchanged, who the closing attorney or escrow should be, whether the seller will assist you with closing cost, and when you are to close and take possession of the home.

Earnest Money

Earnest Money is a certain amount of money which is used as a deposit to show your commitment to purchasing the home. Earnest money becomes a part of your total down payment and closing cost, it is not a separate charge. Earnest money deposit amounts vary according to the region. Your real estate agent will inform you of what is the norm in your area. But earnest money deposits typically range from about $1,000 for an average home to a percentage of the home price. The earnest money check/deposit usually will be held by your agent until the seller accepts your offer at which time it is deposited with the closing attorney or escrow company.

Counter Offer

Is an optional response to your offer, structured with conditions and/ or affirmations to continue negotiations to reach a purchase agreement between the parties.

Once you have found a house for which you want to make an offer, your real estate agent will go over the following information with you to assist you in making an informed decision and deciding on an offer amount.

- Recent home sales in the area

- Market conditions-how quickly homes are selling in the area i.e. days on the market

- The homes' physical condition

- Whether you want or need to negotiate for a seller to pay closing cost

- If you are making an offer on a foreclosure or short sale, do not assume you should automatically offer thousands less than the asking price. Banks have usually accounted for the homes condition in the asking price, and will generally accept 85-90% of asking price unless there are multiple offers. If your real estate agent knows you will be in a multiple offer situation, it is to your benefit to make your best offer initially.

Once you decide your offer amount and other terms your real estate agent will prepare the purchase agreement/offer to purchase. You will need to sign the contract and provide your agent with your earnest money deposit via check, cashier check, or money order.

Your real estate agent will deliver the purchase agreement, pre-approval letter and copy of earnest money deposit to the seller's agent, who will present the offer to the seller.

When presented with your offer the seller may take a day or two to review your offer and has the option of responding in one of the following ways:

- Agree to your offer

- Decline your offer

- Make a counter offer

If the seller responds with a counter-offer, the counter offer will include the seller's desired price and terms. At this point, you can either agree with the terms or structure another counter offer.

This negotiating process continues until you reach an agreement. Keep in mind there are instances where you and the seller may reach an impasse, in which case you will need to move on and look for another house.

Once you have an accepted offer, your real estate agent will begin coordinating your transaction to get you to the closing.

Step 6

❖

During the Transaction

Loan Process

Once you have a binding purchase agreement, your real estate agent will forward a copy of the agreement to your loan officer.

Mortgage Process

Your lender will complete the mortgage application (1003) and request documentation needed to process your loan. You need to provide any requested information as timely as possible as you are now on the clock. You will need to be cooperative as you need to get to closing in a timely manner.

When your documentation is received, your lenders processor will verify and validate that all the information is accurate. Verification request may be sent to your employer, mortgage holder or landlord and banking institutions. It is during this time that the appraisal, title policy, and other inspections are completed.

The processing of your loan can take one to two weeks, but it can be delayed when third parties do not respond to validation request or appraisals are delayed.

Once all the information is collected and verified the loan is then packaged according to lender specifications and sent to the lender's underwriting department.

Mortgage Underwriting

The underwriter has the ultimate power and decision authority over the approval of your loan. Once the underwriter reviews your loan package to make sure it conforms to all the guidelines required for that loan product. They review the appraisal and title report. They may complete additional validation for employment, credit, etc. The underwriting time is determined by a market condition under normal conditions it normally takes 3-5 days. If the market is flooded, it can take up to 2 weeks.

Conditions to Close

When the underwriter is done reviewing your loan she/he will send an "Approval with Conditions" to your loan officer. These are generally just requirements for further documentation to support your loan file. Do not stress yourself with the why do they need this questions. Just remember they are lending you a significant amount of money and provide them with whatever information the lender needs to be made comfortable with lending money to you. When the conditions have been satisfied the underwriter will give a "final loan approval" and "clear to close".

Clear to Close

When you loan officer gets the clear to close, he/she will then schedule and coordinate with your real estate agent and closing attorney/escrow regarding the time and location to sign the final loan documents to close the loan. This can take from one hour to one day.

Draw Documents

When everything is scheduled the lender then draws the loan document package and sends it to the closing attorney/escrow. This can take one to two days.

You are now familiar with what to expect during the mortgage process. Let's talk about the things you **should not do** during the mortgage process. Committing any of these acts can cause your loan to be declined and thus you will not get your home. I like to refer to this list as the **10 commandments of Mortgage loan don't's**.

1. Thou shalt not change or quit your job nor become self-employed.

2. Thou shalt not charge credit cards excessively or let your accounts fall behind.

3. Thou shalt not open new charge cards or buy furniture on credit.

4. Thou shalt not originate new inquiries onto your credit file

5. Thou shalt not buy a new car, truck, van or any vehicle period on credit.

6. Thou shalt not spend money you have set aside for closing.

7. Thou shalt not make large deposits into your bank account without checking with your loan officer first.

8. Thou shalt not change bank accounts.

9. Thou shalt not omit debts or liabilities from your loan application.

10. Thou shalt not co-sign a loan for anyone.

Get A Home Inspection

A home inspection is not a requirement to purchase, it is a choice. The buyer may elect not to have a home inspection. However, aside from the fact that you are making a huge investment, a home inspection helps avoid a costly mistake by purchasing property that needs major repairs, or has significant defects.

With that said, the purpose of the home inspection is not for your to look for a reason to cancel your contract during the contingency period. Rather it is an opportunity for you to learn about the condition of the home and ensure there is no significant or hazardly defects. A home inspection does not determine a home's value.

Upon completion of a home inspection you can submit a request for repairs to the seller, however, keep in mind the seller is **not** required to complete the repairs. Usually, your real estate agent will be able to negotiate with the seller to come to some agreement regarding minor repairs. If the home is sold as is, such as the case with many foreclosures **do not** expect the seller (bank) to complete any repairs. Your inspection has served its purpose in making you aware of the property condition.

Since all purchase agreements allow for a contingency period for you to get inspections completed, if the home is found to have significant defects unrevealed by the seller you will naturally withdraw/cancel your agreement, retrieve your deposit, and resume house hunting.

Finding The Right Home Inspection

It is crucial that you have a qualified home, inspector. Be sure to find an inspector who:

- Have credible references and vast experience
- Is insured and bonded

You may ask for recommendations from your real estate agent and family and friends.

Home inspection cost varies from $250-$650, depending upon location, property, size, and inclusion of optional test.

Your Home Appraisal

A home appraisal is used to determine the fair market value of the property or what is should sell for on the open market. It is not the same as a home inspection.

A home appraisal is required by the mortgage company to ensure the property is worth the amount of money they are lending to you.

If your appraisal comes in low compared with the amount of the loan, your lender will kill the transaction. As they will not lend more than the home is worth nor do yo want to pay more for a home than it's worth. In this instance, your real estate agent can use the appraisal to negotiate with the seller to lower the price to the appraised value. In most instances, this works and however if it does not you have a couple of choices:

- Pay the difference between the appraised value and sales price in cash and continue with the transaction.

- Cancel the transaction according to the appraisal contingency in your contract, get your deposit back and resume house hunting.

The rules surrounding the hiring of appraisers changed after the mortgage crisis.As a result, lenders hire the appraisers via a third party appraisal management company (AMC) to ensure impartiality and reduce the outside influence on appraisal results.

Although, the appraisal fee is a part of your closing cost you will pay for it upfront when the lender makes the request. Appraisal fees generally cost $350 or more depending on location, property type, and market conditions.

An appraisal requires an interior/exterior inspection. The appraiser looks at a number of other factors to determine value such as: the homes condition, age, living space, taxes, neighborhood, views, market conditions, prices of nearby homes (comparables), and future marketability.

Title Insurance and Why You Need It

When you buy a home, you expect to enjoy certain rights and benefits. For example, you expect to occupy and use the home as you wish.To be able to freely sell or pledge your property as security for a loan, and to be free from debts or obligations not created or incurred by you. Title insurance is designed to protect these rights.

The cost of title insurance varies depending on the property value. The most important thing to remember regarding title insurance cost is you only pay once, the coverage continues in effect for as long as you have an interest in the covered property. In the case of death, the coverage automatically continues for the benefit of your heirs. If you sell your property giving warranties of title to your buyer, your coverage continues.Even if a buyer gives you a mortgage to finance the purchase of a covered property from you, your coverage will continue to protect your interest in the property.

At closing you will see two forms of title insurance on your closing documents, the lender's policy covers only the amount of your loan. The owner's policy covers the full value of the property which is why you need both forms of coverage. Title insurance is a small one-time payment for long time piece of mind.

Importance of Home Insurance

Just as no sensible car owner will drive their car without insurance, the same applies to your house. Aside from this statement no lender will complete the mortgage process without you providing homeowners insurance.

Homeowners insurance provides fire, theft, and liability coverage, as well as your personal possessions. Lenders require coverage in an amount at least equal to your loan amount plus 120%.

The best starting point when shopping for your home insurance is with your auto insurance provider, as most insurance companies provide discounts for multiple policies, shop around for the best price and coverage.

Home Warranties

When making an offer, ask you, agent, to request the seller pay for a home warranty. Home warranties are typically single year service agreements. Home warranties help keep unexpected home and appliance cost to a minimum. New construction generally comes with the builder's warranty. There are several different forms of coverage.

After coverage ends, you may elect to continue coverage for as little as $50/month. A very small price to pay for peace of mind.

Final Walk Thru

After disclosures have been exchanged, inspections completed, and the lender has issued a clear to close, it is now time to complete your final walk thru. This is usually done within 5 days of closing. This entire process has usually taken 30-45 days to complete.

The final walk thru **is not** the time to do a home inspection, it is to make sure the condition of the property is the same as it was on the day you signed your offer to purchase. You do not need to verify repairs made due to the home inspection, as by this time those have already been completed. Instead, you are checking a few relevant facts:

- Have areas of the home been damaged? Inspect floors for rips and gouges. Look at walls and around door frames that may have been bumped as large furniture and appliances were moved.

- Make sure all the main systems continue to be in working order.

- If you asked for items to be removed, verify, they are gone.

If the condition has changed since your offer to purchase was accepted, your real estate agent can negotiate repair or replacement funds before or at the closing table.

There are endless scenarios and last minute issues that can delay a closing which is why you need an experienced real estate agent to help you navigate the process. Below is a list I provide to clients of 83 Types of Turbulence, which is basically a list of things that may go wrong. I give them this list ahead of time so if any of these things occur they are already aware and don't freak out as the majority of them can be handled and worked thru.

The 83 Types of Turbulence

The Lender/Closing Attorney:

1. Fails to notify lender/agents of unsigned or unreturned documents.

2. Fails to obtain information from beneficiaries, lien holders, insurance companies, or lenders in a timely manner.

3. Lets principals leave town without getting all necessary signatures.

4. Lost or incorrectly prepares paperwork.

5. Does not pass on valuable information quickly enough.

6. Does not coordinate well, so that many items can be done simultaneously.

7. Does not get HUD to buyer/seller for review and there are errors.

8. Does not find liens or title problems until the last minute.

The Buyer/Borrower:

9. Omits important financial information on the application.

10. Submits incorrect information to the lender.

11. Has recent late payments on credit report.

12. Found out about additional debt after loan application.

13. Borrower loses job.

14. Co-borrower loses job.

15. Income verification lower than what was stated on the loan application.

16. Overtime income not allowed by an underwriter for qualifying.

17. The applicant makes large purchase on credit before closing.

18. Illness, injury, divorce or another financial setback during escrow.

19. Lacks motivation.

20. Gift donor changes mind.

21. Cannot locate divorce decree.

22. Cannot locate petition or discharge of bankruptcy.

23. Cannot locate tax returns. Cannot locate bank statements.

24. Difficulty in obtaining verification of rent.

25. Interest rate increases and borrower no longer qualifies.

26. Loan programs change with higher rates, points, and fees.

27. Child support not disclosed on the application.

28. The borrower is a foreign national.

29. Bankruptcy within the last two years.

30. The mortgage payment is double the previous housing payment.

31. Borrower/co-borrower does not have steady two-year

employment history.

32. Borrower brings in handwritten pay stubs.

33. Borrower switches to a job requiring probation period just before closing.

34. Borrower switches to job from salary to 100% commission income.

35. Borrower/co-borrower/seller dies.

36. Buyer forgets to get INSURANCE BINDER (not needed for condo.)

37. Veterans DD214 form not available.

38. Buyer has spent the money needed for down payment/closing costs, comes up short at closing.

39. The buyer does not properly "paper trail" additional money that comes from gifts, loans, etc.

40. Doesn't bring cashier's check to the closing for down payment/ bank fees.

Seller

41. Loses motivation to sell (job transfer does not go through, reconciles marriage, etc.)

42. Cannot find a suitable replacement property.

43. Will not allow appraiser and inspector inside the home.

44. Seller does not get final water/utility readings for closing attorney.

45. Removes property from the premises the buyer believed was included.

46. Is unable to clear up liens against their property- short on cash to close.

47. Did not own 100% of the property as previously disclosed.

48. Thought getting partners signatures were "no problem," but they were.

49. Leaves town without giving anyone Power of Attorney.

50. Delays the projected move-out date.

51. Did not complete the repairs agreed to in the contract.

52. Seller's home goes into foreclosure during escrow.

53. 54.Does not disclose all hidden or unknown defects and they are subsequently discovered at the home inspection.

54. Builder miscalculates completion date of a new home.

55. Seller has not moved out of the property.

56. Seller is not prepared for the final walk-through of the property.

57. Seller does not appear for closing and won't sign papers.

The Realtor(s):

58. Has bad communication skills.

59. Delays access to the property for inspection and appraisals.

60. Unfamiliar with their client's financial position- do they have enough equity to sell, etc.

61. Does not get completed paperwork to the lender in time.

62. Inexperienced in this type of property transaction.

63. Takes unexpected time off during the transaction and can't be reached.

64. Has huge ego that gets in the way of progress.

65. Does not do sufficient homework on their clients or the property and wastes everyone's time. The Property

66. Board of Health will not approve septic system or well.

67. Inspection report reveals substantial pest damage and the seller is not willing to fix or repair.

68. The home was misrepresented as to size and condition.

69. Home not structurally sound.

70. Home is uninsurable for homeowners insurance

71. Property incorrectly zoned.

72. A portion of the home sits on neighbor's property.

The Appraiser

73. Is not local and misunderstands the market.

74. Is too busy to complete the appraisal on schedule.

75. No comparable sales are available.

76. Is not on the lender's "approved list."

77. Makes significant mistakes on appraisal and brings in value too low.

78. Lender requires a second or "review" appraisal.

Inspectors

79. Inspector too busy to schedule inspection when needed.

80. Inspector isnot experienced in representing the accurate condition of the property.

81. Home inspector not available when needed.

82. Inspection reports alarm buyer and sale is canceled.

Step 7

❖

Prepare For Closing

It's been 30-45 days since you found a home your love and signed your purchase agreement. The time has come to close.

The first thing I want you to remember is not to stress about the closing date. 90% of real estate transactions do not close on the exact closing date stated in the contract, most are a few days late.

There are a few things you need to do to prepare for closing.

- Verify whether the seller has completely vacated the home as scheduled. Otherwise, you need to negotiate rent payments.

- Call utility companies a few days in advance to transfer service, however, some may request proof of ownership before transferring service.

- Do not give your landlord a move outdate until you have a clear to close from your underwriter.

Once you closing attorney/escrow company receives your loan documents from your lender. The closer will provide you with an estimated settlement statement (HUD-1) form. The settlement will itemize all your closing cost and fees. You and your real estate agent should review the estimated settlement statement to ensure the closing cost and fees are correct. The settlement statement should also be compared to good faith estimate you were given at the beginning of the loan application. The fees will not match exactly, but there should be no huge discrepancies. Upon receipt of loan documents the

- Closing Attorney/Escrow will contact you to schedule your closing appointment.

- Your Estimated Settlement Statement(HUD-1) will indicate the balance of your down payment and closing cost needed to purchase your home. These funds will need to be bought into the Closing Attorney/Escrow at the closing appointment. The funds need to be certified funds, which for this purpose is a cashier check or wire. If you wire funds arrange to have funds wired the day before or first thing the morning of closing. The cashier check or wire must come from the bank account used to obtain your mortgage. For closing purposes, you can not use cash, checks or money orders.

Step 8

❖

Close and Move-In

On the day of your closing, you will need to bring a valid identification card and certified check (unless you wired funds ahead), and any documentation that may be deemed required by the closing agent.

In states that close with an escrow company, it is not uncommon for the buyer to attend the closing by his or herself.

In states that close with an attorney the buyer may attend by themselves or with your real estate agent, the seller agent and or the sellers may sometimes also attend.

Signing Your Closing Documents

Be ready to sign your name 75-100 times. You will sign your final mortgage loan and other closing documents. The most important of these documents are:

Mortgage Note

A promissory note that is basically an IOU that contains the promise to pay the loan as well as the terms of repayment. The note includes the:

- Name of borrower

- Property address

- Amount of the loan

- Interest rate (indicates fixed or adjustable)

- Late charge amount

- Term (number of years)

The note is not recorded in the county land records. The lender holds the note while the loan is outstanding. When the loan is fully paid off, the note will be marked as paid in full and returned to the borrower.

Deeds of Trust

The deed of trust provides security for the loan that is evidenced by a promissory note.

Along with the standard covenants between the borrower and the lender, the deed of trust will contain an acceleration clause that permits the lender to demand that the entire balance of the loan be repaid if the borrower defaults on the loan (by not making payments for example). If the borrower does not make the payments due on the promissory note, then the property can be foreclosed and sold to satisfy the debt.

The will contain the following information:

- Name of borrower

- Property address

- Legal description of the property

The deed of trust is recorded in the county land records, shortly after the borrower signs it.

When the loan is paid off, the lender will record a reconveyance of deed (satisfaction) in the county land records.

You have signed your loan and closing documents and provided your closing funds.

"CONGRATULATIONS YOU'RE A
HOMEOWNER!!!"

Other Books by Tonya Brown

The Road to BLISSS-My Dysfunctional Relationship With
Money and How I Found BLISSS (Available November 2015)

Buy Your First Home Using The Government's
Money(Available November 2015)

About Tonya Brown

Things I live by:
God and family first. Always be thankful. Never be afraid of change. Keep it pushing. Never give up. Move forward. Never stop learning. We create ourselves by the choices we make.

Thank you for taking the time to read my book, here is a little about me:

I am a mother, New Age grandmother. An avid reader (I devour 5-6 books/month). A fabulous cook, fashionista, and sometimes a diva. I enjoy traveling and renovating homes. I enjoy learning and educating others.

I am the Broker/Owner of Blisss Life Realty in Atlanta, GA. I have been a mortgage and real estate broker since 1997. I am the founder and CEO of Blisss Life Enterprises that consist of 3 brands:

- Blisss Life Realty, a full-service residential estate brokerage offering a first class experience.

- Blisss Life, a wealth building brand dedicating to educating African American millennials learn to respect money so that they can live a financially free, blisssful life.

- Rehab-Renew Travel, offering a first-class travel experience.

www.ingramcontent.com/pod-product-compliance
Lightning Source LLC
Chambersburg PA
CBHW070819210326
41520CB00011B/2019